INTRODUCTION

This book contains over 150 mazes, including every maze from **A-MAZE-ING Animals**, **Myths and Monsters**, and **Maze-o-zoic**! In these pages, you will find dogs, dragons, dinosaurs, and so much more. Not only that, there are also ten brand new mazes never before seen in any book. Part of the fun is not just solving the puzzles, but discovering all the colorful creatures on each and every page.

The mazes have been given difficulty levels from 1 to 5. You can start with a level 1 and work your way up to 5, or feel free to solve the mazes randomly. The difficulty level is determined by how long it should take to solve the maze. A level 5 maze might be perfect for the car ride to Grandma's house, but a quick level 1 might be just right before bedtime.

Mazes start at the start and finish at the finish—doesn't that make sense? But it's not quite that simple. Sometimes there are multiple paths leading out from the **START** and most of the **FINISH** points have several paths leading out as well (for those sneaky kids who like to start from the finish!).

Choose your paths wisely. Take your time. Try not to get frustrated. If you get stumped on a maze, take a break and come back to it later. If you get really, really stumped, the solutions are in the back of the book, but try not to peek!

So pick up a pencil and settle in to have some **A-MAZE-ING** fun as you navigate the mazes from start to finish!

PUBLISHING

1

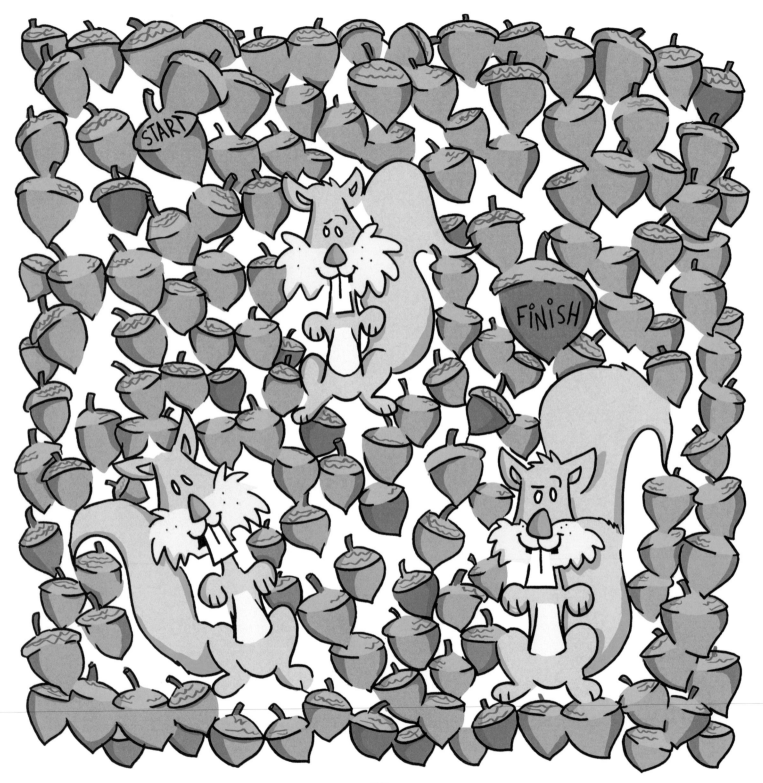

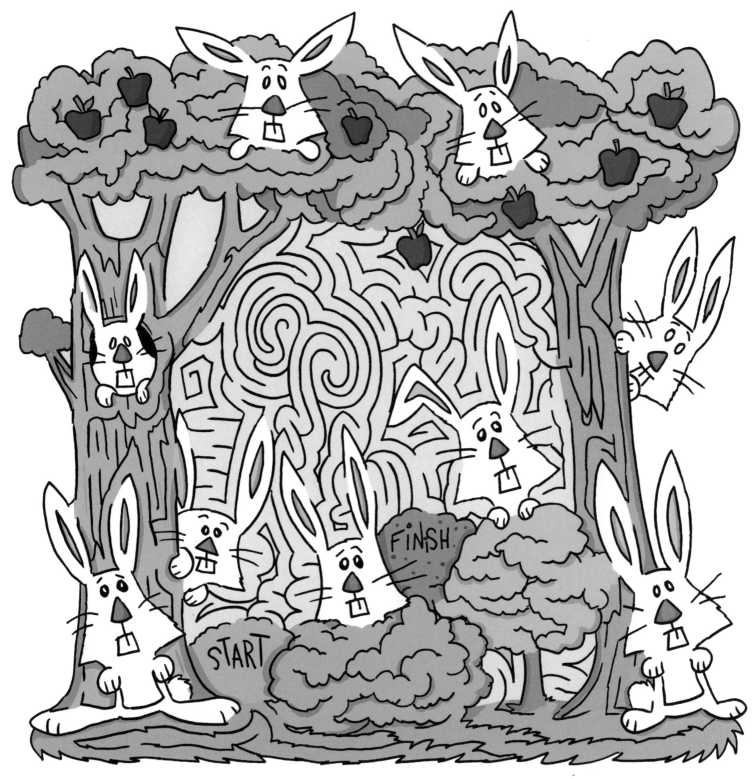

START

FINISH

FINISH

START

FINISH

START

FINISH

START

START

FINISH

START

FINISH

START

FINISH

Solutions

Page 2

Page 3

Page 4

Page 5

162

Solutions

Page 6

Page 7

Page 8

Page 9

Solutions

Page 10

Page 11

Page 12

Page 13

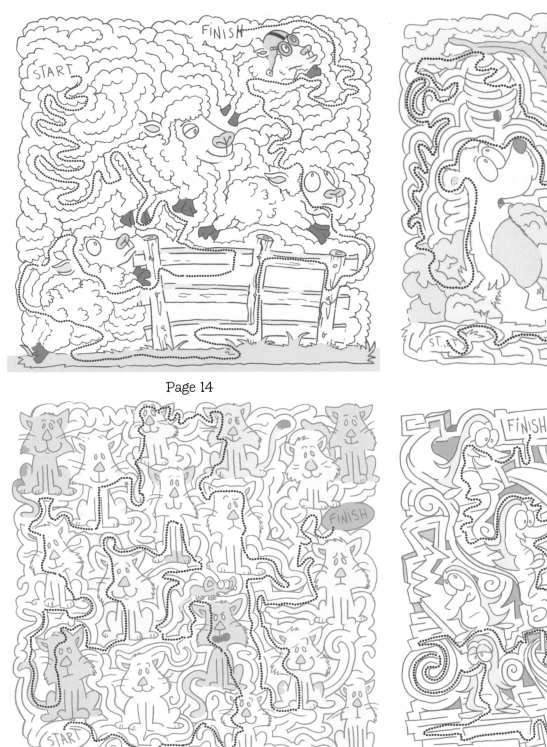

Page 14

Page 15

Page 16

Page 17

Solutions

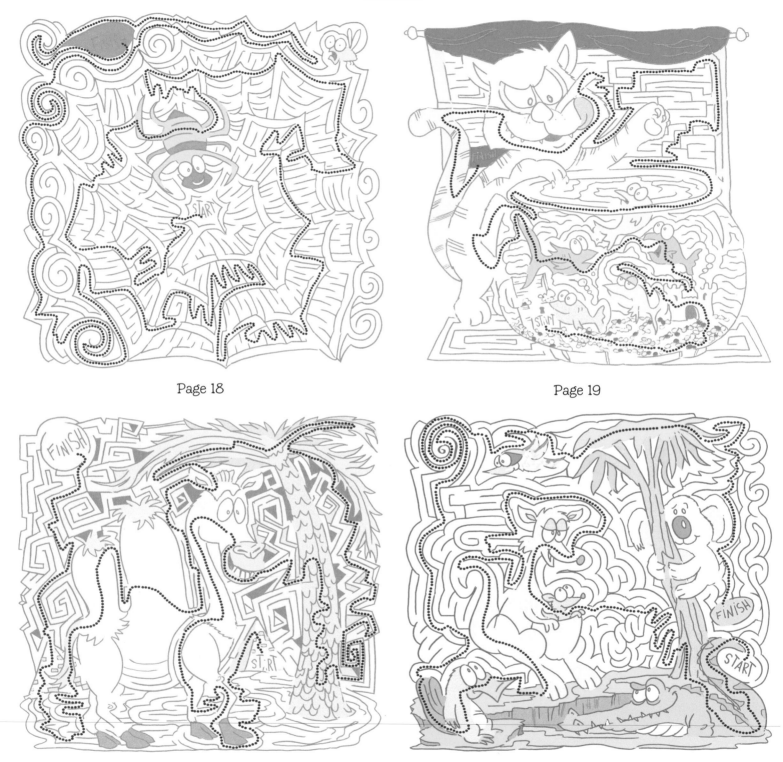

Page 18

Page 19

Page 20

Page 21

Solutions

Page 22

Page 23

Page 24

Page 25

Solutions

Page 26

Page 27

Page 28

Page 29

Page 30

Page 31

Page 32

Page 33

Solutions

Page 34

Page 35

Page 36

Page 37

Page 38

Page 39

Page 40

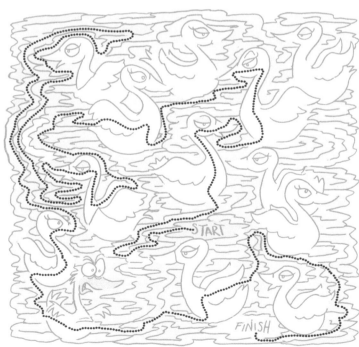

Page 41

Solutions

Page 42

Page 43

Page 44

Page 45

Page 46

Page 47

Page 48

Page 49

Page 50

Page 51

Page 52

Page 53

Page 54

Page 55

Page 56

Page 57

Solutions

Page 58

Page 59

Page 60

Page 61

Page 62

Page 63

Page 64

Page 65

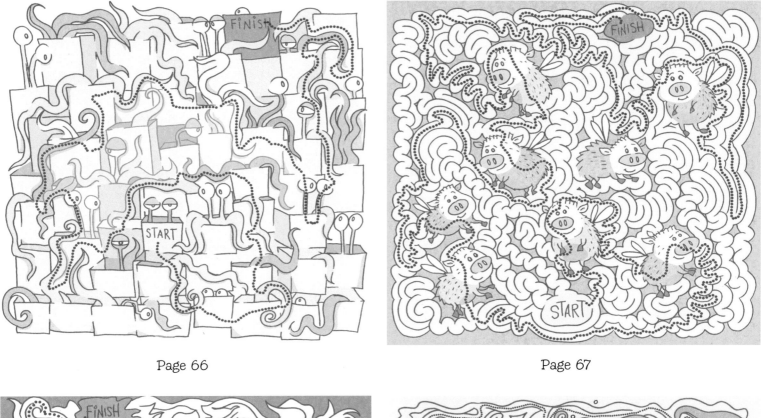

Page 66

Page 67

Page 68

Page 69

Page 70

Page 71

Page 72

Page 73

Page 74

Page 75

Page 76

Page 77

Page 78

Page 79

Page 80

Page 81

Page 82

Page 83

Page 84

Page 85

Page 86

Page 87

Page 88

Page 89

Page 90

Page 91

Page 92

Page 93

Page 94

Page 95

Page 96

Page 97

Page 98

Page 99

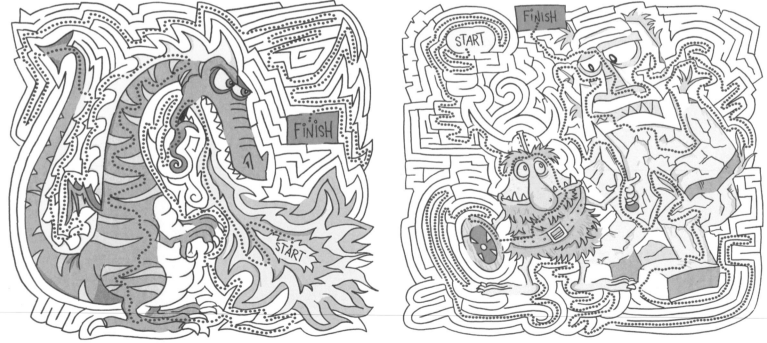

Page 100

Page 101

Page 102

Page 103

Page 104

Page 105

Solutions

Page 106

Page 107

Page 108

Page 109

Page 110

Page 111

Page 112

Page 113

Page 114

Page 115

Page 116

Page 117

Page 118

Page 119

Page 120

Page 121

Solutions

Page 122

Page 123

Page 124

Page 125

Page 126

Page 127

Page 128

Page 129

Solutions

Page 130

Page 131

Page 132

Page 133

Solutions

Page 134

Page 135

Page 136

Page 137

Solutions

Page 138

Page 139

Page 140

Page 141

Solutions

Page 142

Page 143

Page 144

Page 145

Page 146

Page 147

Page 148

Page 149

Page 150

Page 151

Page 152

Page 153

Page 154

Page 155

Page 156

Page 157

Page 158

Page 159

Page 160

Page 161

All inquiries should be addressed to:
Peterson's Publishing, LLC
4380 S. Syracuse Street, Suite 200
Denver, CO 80237-2624
www.petersonsbooks.com

ISBN: 978-1-4380-8925-6

Date of Manufacture: February 2021
Manufactured by: WKT, Shenzhen, China

Printed in China
9 8 7 6 5 4 3 2 1